# China's Expanding Role in Global Mergers and Acquisitions Markets

Charles Wolf, Jr., Brian G. Chow,
Gregory S. Jones, Scott Harold

RAND CENTER FOR ASIA PACIFIC POLICY

International Programs at RAND

The research described in this report was conducted within the RAND Center for Asia Pacific Policy (CAPP) under the auspices of the International Programs of the RAND Corporation.

Library of Congress Control Number: 2011942985

ISBN: 978-0-8330-5968-0

The RAND Corporation is a nonprofit institution that helps improve policy and decisionmaking through research and analysis. RAND's publications do not necessarily reflect the opinions of its research clients and sponsors.

**RAND®** is a registered trademark.

Published 2011 by the RAND Corporation
1776 Main Street, P.O. Box 2138, Santa Monica, CA 90407-2138
1200 South Hayes Street, Arlington, VA 22202-5050
4570 Fifth Avenue, Suite 600, Pittsburgh, PA 15213-2665
RAND URL: http://www.rand.org/
To order RAND documents or to obtain additional information, contact
Distribution Services: Telephone: (310) 451-7002;
Fax: (310) 451-6915; Email: order@rand.org

# Preface

During the coming decade, China will play an increasingly influential role in global capital markets. This role will be powered by large and sustained surpluses in China's current accounts—that is, the excess of China's earnings over its payments in international transactions. Some of these surpluses will be invested in acquiring ownership or partial ownership of foreign companies and other assets, including some in the United States. It is timely and important for U.S. analysts to understand the underlying strategy and the attendant consequences—both favorable and unfavorable—that may be associated with these investments.

The research described in this monograph analyzed recent and proposed Chinese investments in U.S. companies, including both acquisitions that were completed and ones that were disallowed or withdrawn. The research also reviewed China's recent and prospective investments in companies in Europe, Asia, and the rest of the world. The aim of this review was to gain an understanding of China's investment patterns and to develop a methodology to improve the assessment of whether proposed investments should be allowed or should require measures to mitigate risk. Data used in the monograph cover the decade through 2009, with occasional references to 2010. Many of the trends and forecasts drawn from these data have been reinforced by more recent data.

This research was conducted within the RAND Center for Asia Pacific Policy, part of International Programs at the RAND Corporation. The center aims to improve public policy by providing decisionmakers and the public with rigorous, objective research on critical policy issues affecting Asia and U.S.-Asia relations.

For more information on the RAND Center for Asia Pacific Policy, see http://www.rand.org/international_programs/capp/ or contact the director (contact information is provided on the web page).

# Contents

# Figures and Tables

## Figures

## Tables

# Summary

## Background and Scope

One of the few propositions on which virtually all China experts agree is that foreign investment *in* China has been a major contributor to the Chinese economy's remarkable growth over the past three decades. In addition to the direct benefits realized from the invested capital itself—which increased more than sixfold between 1992 and 2007— significant additional benefits accrued indirectly from the technology, management, and marketing skills that were associated with foreign investment.

From China's perspective, these large capital inflows were sometimes viewed as entailing risks that were mitigated by imposing restrictions on foreign investment. These measures included limiting foreign equity investment to nonvoting "B" shares, constraining the proportion of ownership that foreign investors could acquire in Chinese companies, and limiting the number and size of foreign firms' financial platforms in China's capital markets.

In the coming decade, foreign investments *by* China may become an important contributor to growth in the rest of the world, as well as a major factor in global mergers-and-acquisitions markets. Besides the direct effects of prospective investments from China, there also will be indirect benefits realized through improved know-how, learning, and market access relating to local procedures and regulations within China's 37 diverse provinces and administrative regions. From the perspectives of recipients of China's foreign investments, there may also be concerns and risks. These risks may entail the broad national interests, sensitive technologies, and natural resources of countries receiving China's investments. Recipient countries may thus seek to mitigate these risks through various measures discussed in this monograph.

In this monograph, we seek to improve understanding of China's foreign investment patterns and strategy. We explicitly consider whether and how U.S. national interests might be compromised by some of China's investments and how these interests can be safeguarded without interfering with, indeed by encouraging, opportunities for investments that advance the economic interests of the United States, other countries, and China.

Our research focused on China's investments in U.S. companies and, more particularly, investments in U.S. companies whose acquisition by China might affect U.S. national security. This focus entailed paying special attention to prior investments by China that led to reviews by the United States as well as to potential investments that might warrant such assessments in the future. The research also sought to compare China's investments in the United States with those of several top-rated private equity (PE) companies to provide a benchmark for evaluating their respective similarities and differences, as well as their patterns and inferred priorities. A fuller understanding of China's investment strategy also required looking more broadly at China's investments in countries other than the United States and considering how China's investments in the United States fit into this broader pattern. Consequently, the research described in this monograph also provides an initial examination of the pattern of China's investments in Europe, Asia, and the rest of the world, and inferences that may be drawn from this wider view of China's foreign investment strategy.

## China, the United States, and the Global Economy

In the evolving global economy, China's large and growing financial resources will strengthen its bargaining power when it looks for companies and resources abroad. The resulting challenge for both target investment countries and China is how to nurture the opportunities for and potential benefits from efficient allocation of Chinese investments while avoiding or sharply limiting possible risks to national security in the countries of proposed investments. The implied goal of this research is to develop policies and procedures that will promote win-win outcomes while minimizing outcomes that might involve losses for the countries involved.

The drivers of China's remarkable economic growth during the past three decades have included both direct investment from abroad as well as massive domestic investment constituting more than 35 percent of China's gross domestic product (GDP), an unprecedentedly high domestic savings rate of 45 percent of GDP, continued growth of both labor productivity and total factor productivity, and open and expanding markets for China's exports, especially to the United States until mid-2008. These drivers have also included important institutional changes in China: privatization of state-owned enterprises, vigorously competitive domestic product markets, volatile and sometimes highly speculative securities markets, emergent attention to corporate governance, and serious if imperfectly effective efforts to control corruption.

As a consequence of these multiple drivers, China has become the world's second-largest economy. As its economy has grown, China has accumulated the world's largest holdings of foreign exchange reserves—over $2.1 trillion at the start of 2010, one-third larger than those of Japan. These huge holdings enable China to expand its foreign investments and to seek and acquire companies and other assets abroad.

China's increased prominence in the evolving global economy also stems from its bilateral economic relations with the United States; the effects of the global financial crisis on these relations, including the respective fiscal stimulus programs in both China and the United States; and the consequences of these matters for China's recent and prospective investments in U.S. companies, as well as in countries and companies in other parts of the world. China's increasing prominence in the world economy has led to some discussion of possible reforms to the international financial system in which the yuan would become a generally accepted international reserve currency. Such reforms are unlikely in the short to medium term because the yuan's prospects as a reserve currency will be remote as long as it remains incompletely convertible. China's policymakers have repeatedly stipulated that capital transactions are unlikely to be fully convertible for the indefinite future. In the longer run, the prospects are brighter.

## China's Recent and Prospective Foreign Investments

China's broad foreign investment strategy appears to be distinctive, selective, and flexible—characteristics that we discuss in Chapter Three.

It is distinctive in that it reflects both the central government and ruling party's broad national priorities that prominently include the salient need of the Chinese economy to sustain high rates of economic growth. This distinctive role of the central government results from the fact that China's major foreign capital transactions require approval of the State Assets Board (SAB) and the State Administration for Foreign Exchange (SAFE), which are accountable to the State Council. When competing claims arise for using China's foreign investments to help meet the demands of the economy, the military, or the economy's technological advancement, these claims are resolved by the institutions at the top of the institutional pyramid. The distinctiveness of China's investment strategy is also reflected in the contrast between Chinese investments in recent years and investments made in the same period by several prominent global PE firms: Blackstone, Kohlberg-Kravis-Roberts, Carlyle, Cerberus, and Berkshire Hathaway.

That China's investment strategy is selective is evident from the conspicuous differences between China's investments in the United States and its investments in Europe, Asia, and the rest of the world during the 2007–2009 period. Selectivity is also reflected by the fact that China's foreign investments sometimes focus on realizing stable returns or realizing higher if more volatile returns; whereas in other instances, the focus is on acquiring companies with large oil, gas, and other mineral resource holdings or companies with advanced technology, laboratories, and testing capabilities; and in still other instances, the companies China has acquired are ones with evident financial experience, connections, and know-how.

That the strategy is flexible is suggested by recent policy pronouncements by top Chinese leaders expressing encouragement for expanded Chinese investment abroad, especially by China's most "capable" companies, including state-owned enterprises, while adopting a more restrictive stance toward ones judged less capable.

Notwithstanding frequent Chinese criticism of mounting U.S. budget deficits and the jeopardy this creates for the stability of the U.S. dollar, China's investments in the United States continue to be predominantly in U.S. Treasury notes and bills and other government obligations. China's accumulation of these government assets by the middle of 2009 reached $1.5 trillion, of which nearly one-third was accumulated from 2007 through the middle of 2009. Apart from these investments, China's investments in U.S. companies in the same period were small, amounting to $25.8 billion, and were concentrated in the financial and business services fields. The reasons for this concentration include China's (plausible but mistaken) expectation of high rates of return on investments in these sectors, as well as the reasonable expectation by China's policymakers that such acquisitions would provide an opportunity to learn about and to access information on the broadest spectrum of companies throughout the U.S. economy.

We expect the scale of China's investments in U.S. companies to rise in the next few years and the pattern to shift from finance and business services. The reasons for this forecast include China's continued accumulation of large current account surpluses, emergent opportunities for acquiring a wider range of U.S companies as a result of their depressed valuations, the expanding needs of the Chinese economy for high technology, and a growing belief that receptivity in the United States to acquisitions by financially well-endowed Chinese investors may be somewhat higher than in prior years.

Our comparison of China's investments in U.S. companies with investments made by the selected PE firms highlights the sharp differences in their respective investment patterns. For example, the five PE firms as a group invested most heavily in hotels and motels, real estate, construction materials, motor vehicles, and packaged frozen foods during the 2007–2009 period of the great recession. In sharp contrast, Chinese investments in the same period were concentrated in financial and business services, with smaller stakes in electronics, telecommunications, and medical equipment. In turn, the differing investment patterns reflect the differing business models and differing objectives attributed to each: for China, seeking to meet the expanding needs associated with its aggressive growth and geostrategic interests; for the PE firms, seeking to acquire, enhance, and resell companies at high rates of return in the short to medium term.

Turning to China's investments in Europe in the 2007–2009 period, we have only made an initial, cursory effort to collect and analyze the data. We find that China's investments in Europe concentrated in two sectors during that period: namely, minority acquisitions in multinational oil and gas companies and in financial and banking services. The focus on oil and gas reflects the priority accorded to "resource security" by China's policymakers—a theme that is also dominant in China's investments in Asia and the rest of the world. However, in the European context, the oil and gas priority takes the form of acquiring minority shares in some of the large global multinational producers, whereas in Asia and the rest of the world, the same priority leads to investments aimed at acquiring either full ownership stakes or major stakes in production companies.

We also expect China's investments in Europe to expand as a consequence of China's continuing large current account surpluses. The broadened scope of China's European investments may be affected as well by China's anticipation that acquisitions of high-technology companies may encounter less sensitivity and resistance than similarly targeted acquisitions might encounter in the United States.

China's investments in Asia and the rest of the world show a markedly different pattern from its investments in the United States and Europe. In Asia and the rest of the world, China's investments have concentrated on resource industries, such as oil, gas, copper, iron, lead, and zinc. Moreover, the small $18 billion of China's investments in Asia and the rest of the world in the 2007–2009 period tracked in our study excludes substantial additional lending (i.e., $35 billion) by Chinese financial institutions to resource industries in Brazil and Singapore, as well as additional long-term procurement contracts in Iran and

Libya for oil and gas and other resources. These financial commitments may, in some instances, lead to investment acquisitions in the future.

The increasing emphasis on resource investments in these areas is likely to continue in the coming years, as well as grow in scale.

It is not clear whether this policy is wise or optimal, for reasons on both sides of this issue that are discussed more fully in the body of the monograph.

## Assessing Proposed or Potential Chinese Investments in Other Countries

In considering the effects of foreign investments in the United States, we employ a broad definition of these terms, to include those technologies and services pertinent to economic security and economic growth, not limiting these definitions to the traditional and narrower meanings related to national defense. To develop the methodology, we reviewed 20 proposed Chinese investments from 2000 to 2008 and then refined the design by considering four additional cases to illustrate the framework. We then turned to the development of a way to assess the broader national security implications of possible future Chinese investments in financial and business services and in energy.[1]

The analytic methodology, schematized in Figure S.1, consists of a modified decision-tree analysis involving a series of steps sometimes considered simultaneously, at other times considered sequentially.

As the schematic suggests, the methodology describes a process whose successive stops enable the criticality of technology acquisitions to be judged and also shows the status of the potential acquirer to be assessed, whether a national security risk is thereby entailed, whether a mitigation plan can abate such risk, and whether the potential acquirer would have ready access to alternatives to accomplish the same purposes as sought from the acquisition under review.

---

[1]   Other sectors can be examined using the same analytic framework.

**Figure S.1**
**Steps for Assessing National Security Risks and Benefits from Foreign Investments**

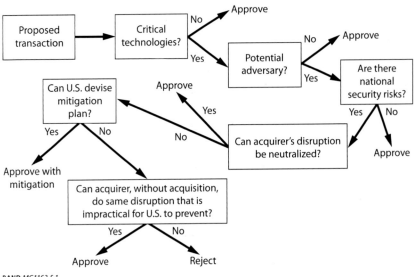

RAND *MG1162-S.1*

This process also results in certain guidelines for assessing possible future bids and proposals by China. In developing these guidelines, we invoke the principle of reciprocity between China's treatment of foreign investments in China and potential treatment by other countries of China's investments in them. We suggest that reciprocity can be invoked without compromising a general preference for open and competitive capital markets. Furthermore, the assessment of risks should be accompanied by a separate assessment of potential benefits from any such acquisition, examining the associated benefits in light of the broadened definition of critical technologies referred to above.

## Conclusions, Implications, and Guidelines for Further Research

In the evolving world economy, China's large and growing financial resources are propelled by the world's largest trade balances and the largest current account balances—trends that may diminish somewhat but are likely to continue during the next half-dozen years or more. The result will increase China's influence in the global economy and strengthen its bargaining power as it seeks companies and resources abroad, including those in the United States.

As both a consequence of and contributor to these trends, China's attempts and success in making additional investments in U.S. companies are likely to grow substantially in the coming years. Most of its acquisitions are likely to be mutually beneficial to the United States and to China. Where they may not be beneficial, the analytic methodology we have developed can help to improve understanding and to provide guidelines for further investigation and analysis of such acquisitions.

From discussions within the United States and with China, we concluded that it is important to recall and to invoke the principle of reciprocity in devising mitigation plans to arrive at win-win outcomes, while avoiding losses to either party. During the past two decades, China has acquired considerable experience in both encouraging and circumscribing foreign, including U.S., investments in China. Reciprocity would require cooperative and compliant response by China to creative mitigation plans by the United States or other countries for any proposed acquisitions of companies that may entail potential security risks.

Finally, a "wider-angle lens" would be valuable in tracking China's foreign investments. China's investments in European companies should be viewed with a lens that is no less acute than the one applied to viewing China's acquisition of U.S. companies. This also applies to China's investments in Asia and in the rest of the world. In recent years, these investments have mainly been in resource industries, including oil, gas, copper, iron, lead, and zinc. In turn, China's focus on "resource security" is viewed within China as deriving from the high priority that China accords to economic growth and its presumed requirement for secure supplies of critical materials. The wisdom of this policy is open to serious questions which we address in this monograph. Also open to question is whether China's efforts to expand such investments in Asia and the rest of the world may be as likely to benefit, as to harm, the United States as another principal importer of oil, gas, copper, iron, lead, and zinc. The wider-angle lens for viewing China's investment acquisitions in resource fields can also help to anticipate whether and when a series of Chinese investments might lead to acquisition of quasi-monopoly power over valuable ores and other resources, which, in turn, might create vulnerabilities for the economy and national security in the United States and other countries.

# Acknowledgments

The authors gratefully acknowledge the informed, thoughtful, and invaluable comments we received in the detailed reviews of earlier drafts of this work by RAND colleagues Howard Shatz and Krishna Kumar. We carefully considered their comments, many of which we incorporated in revisions made in earlier drafts. For some of their comments, we retain an agreement to disagree, while fully absolving the reviewers of any responsibility for the views expressed and the conclusions reached in the monograph.

The monograph has also benefited from careful and thorough editing by Patricia Bedrosian.

Finally, Barbara Neff, Roberta Shanman, and Anita Szafran have provided us with innumerable library services in data collection and in checking sources and references—all of these done with the speed, reliability, and professionalism that characterize their work.

# Abbreviations

CDB      China Development Bank

CIC      China Investment Corporation

CITIC    China International Trust and Investment Corporation

CNOOC    China National Offshore Oil Corporation

CNPC     China National Petroleum Corporation

FDI      foreign direct investment

FINSA    Foreign Investment and National Security Act of 2007

GDP      gross domestic product

ICBC     Industrial and Commercial Bank of China

IMF      International Monetary Fund

KKR      Kohlberg-Kravis-Roberts

NSC      National Security Council

PE       private equity

P.L.     Public Law

SAB      State Assets Board

SAFE     State Administration for Foreign Exchange

SDR      special drawing rights

SIC        Standard Industrial Code

U.S.C.     United States Code

# CHAPTER ONE

# Background and Objectives

One of the few propositions on which virtually all China experts—inside as well as outside China—agree is that foreign investment *in* China has been a major contributor to the Chinese economy's remarkable growth over the past several decades. Between 1992 and 2007, annual foreign investment in China increased sixfold, from $11 billion to $70 billion—a growth that reflected both investment opportunities and their anticipated benefits.[1] In addition to the direct benefits realized from the invested capital itself—whether through joint ventures or equity investment—significant additional benefits accrued indirectly from the technology, management, and marketing that were associated with these investments.[2]

From China's perspective, these large capital inflows entailed risks, which China's policymakers addressed through various means. Their

---

[1] The sixfold increase refers to foreign direct investment (FDI), sometimes contrasted with portfolio investment. The former is cross-border investment that involves control or influence over a company and can take place through a variety of means; the latter involves cross-border positions in equity or debt securities not intended to give the investor control or influence over the foreign company. A common feature of FDI is that the foreign investor directly owns equity that entitles it to 10 percent or more of the voting power in the foreign company. Much recent and prospective foreign investment by China involves acquisition of all or majority shares of entire companies; hence, it is FDI.

[2] See Charles Wolf, Jr., K. C. Yeh, Benjamim Zycher, Nicholas Eberstadt, and Sung-Ho Lee, *Fault Lines in China's Economic Terrain,* Santa Monica, Calif.: RAND Corporation, MR-1686-NA/SRF, 2003, pp. 141–156; Shuxun Chen and Charles Wolf, Jr., *China, the United States, and the Global Economy,* Santa Monica, Calif.: RAND Corporation, MR-1300-RC, 2001, pp. 147–192; Yasheng Huang, *Selling China: Foreign Direct Investment During the Reform Era,* Cambridge, UK: Cambridge University Press, 2003.

risk-mitigation measures included restricting foreign equity investment to nonvoting "B" shares, constraining the proportion of ownership that foreign investors could acquire in Chinese companies, and limiting the number and size of foreign firms' financial platforms in China's capital markets.

In the coming decade, investments abroad *by* China may become a significant element in global capital markets, a major factor in mergers and acquisitions markets, and an important contributor to growth in other parts of the world, as well as a source of both direct and indirect benefits for China that are linked to these investments. For example, as a consequence of such investments, China's diverse 37 provinces and administrative regions may learn how to improve business management and corporate governance in their domestic markets.

From the perspectives of potential recipients, China's foreign investments may also entail risks. These risks may embrace broad national interests, sensitive and newly emergent technologies, and the natural resources of countries receiving China's investments. Hence, recipient countries are likely to constrain such risks through various means, which we will discuss below. Doubtless, too, China's foreign investments will be associated with a general expansion of Chinese influence in the global economy during the coming decade.

The research described in this report has two aims. The first is to improve understanding of China's foreign investment patterns and strategy. The second is to develop a methodology for evaluating whether China's proposed foreign investments should be approved or modified based upon considerations of both national security interests as well as economic consequences.

Chapter Two provides a brief account of the international economic and financial environment as context for what is addressed in subsequent chapters.

Chapter Three reviews China's recent and prospective foreign investments. It compares China's investments in the United States with those of several top-rated private equity (PE) firms. Comparing and contrasting China's investments in the United States with those of several major private equity firms helps to highlight the differences that in fact predominate, as well as perhaps to indicate some similarities in their respective investment patterns and implicit priorities, thereby providing a basis for inferences about, and a better understanding of, China's foreign investment strategy. To gain a better understanding of China's investment strategy required looking more broadly at China's investments in other parts of the world to see how its investments in the United States may fit into this broader pattern.

In common with other large economies—especially those that are growing and aspire to sustain growth—China's foreign investments are heavily influenced by China's domestic economic interests as well as its security interests. As these shift, along with cyclical and structural domestic and international conditions and perhaps domestic political conditions as well, the pattern and priorities of foreign investments are likely also to change. An overview of our initial research on the pattern of China's global investments is included in Chapter Three.

In Chapter Four, we develop and discuss a methodology that could be further developed to help assess whether or not future proposed investments by China, or other countries, should be approved or whether conditions might be placed on these investments to mitigate risk, considering both national security implications and economic benefits.

Our conclusions and implications are summarized in Chapter Five.

# CHAPTER TWO

# China, the United States, and the Global Economy

In the evolving global economy, China's large and growing financial resources will strengthen its ability to seek companies and resources abroad. This leverage will predictably encounter resistance for political and security as well as economic reasons. The resulting challenge for both target investment countries and China is how to nurture the opportunities for and potential benefits from efficient allocation of Chinese foreign investments while avoiding or minimizing risks to the national security and other interests of the United States and other recipient countries. The goal of this research is to develop an understanding of these investments and a methodology to review them that will promote decisions conducive to win-win outcomes while minimizing outcomes that involve losses.

China's economy has maintained annual gross domestic product (GDP) growth in the neighborhood of 9 to 10 percent during the past decade through 2008.[1] Principal drivers behind this remarkable record have included, besides the foreign direct investment referred to above, a large, low-cost labor supply and a growing component of skilled labor; massive domestic investment constituting more than 35 percent of GDP and underpinned by extraordinarily high domestic savings rates of 45 percent of GDP; continued growth of factor productivity (i.e., productivity of both labor and capital); and open and expanding mar-

---

[1] "Neighborhood" is intended to cover a variety of questions concerning the reliability of data pertaining to China's economic growth and more particularly the comparability of time series data, which, for example, may include in later years components not equivalently covered in earlier years. See for example, Thomas G. Rawski, "What's Happening to China's GDP Statistics?" *China Economic Review*, Vol. 12, No. 4, December 2001.

kets for China's exports, especially in the United States, until mid-2008 when economic decline struck the United States and the global economy.

The drivers have also included important institutional changes, in addition to the cited quantitative ones. The contributing institutional changes included pervasive privatization of state-owned enterprises that formerly dominated and burdened the Chinese economy; vigorously competitive domestic markets, including sometimes excessively volatile and speculative securities markets; emergent attention to more effective corporate governance; and serious if imperfectly effective efforts to rout out corruption.[2]

These multiple drivers have made China the world's second-largest economy, after the United States and ahead of Japan.[3] As its economy has grown, China has accumulated the world's largest holdings of foreign exchange reserves, currently about $2.1 trillion, one-third larger than those of Japan.[4] Held jointly by China's central bank (the People's Bank of China), the State Administration for Foreign Exchange (SAFE), and the State Assets Board (SAB), these resources enable China to expand its foreign investments by acquiring companies and other assets abroad.

China's past and continuing accumulation of foreign exchange reserves reflects perennial surpluses on its global current accounts, including its bilateral surpluses with the United States; the latter constitute about two-thirds of the former. Until recently, these current account surpluses have consisted mainly of China's trade surplus: the excess of China's exports of goods and services over its imports. But, the composition of China's continuingly large current account surpluses is changing. In the first five years of the 21st century, China's global trade surpluses constituted 85–90 percent of its total current

---

[2]  See, for example, William H. Overholt, *The Rise of China: How Economic Reform Is Creating a New Superpower*, London and New York: W. W. Norton & Company, Inc., 1993; Huang, 2003.

[3]  World Bank, *World Bank Indicators Database*, September 15, 2009a; World Bank, *World Bank Indicators Database*, October 7, 2009b.

[4]  To see how the authors arrived at these estimates, see footnote 4 in Chapter Three.

account surpluses. In 2008 and 2009, the trade component shrank to less than 70 percent of China's global current account surplus, with the remainder consisting mainly of earnings from its accumulated foreign investments, including those in the United States.

The significance of this change lies in the fact that China has come to rely more on net earnings from its foreign investments (over and above earnings accruing to foreign investors in China) and somewhat less on its trade balance. Hence, achieving high returns on its foreign investments becomes of increased importance as a means of providing financing for China's further foreign acquisitions. This change is likely to continue and to grow if and as China focuses more policy attention on investing abroad.

In bilateral transactions with the United States, as distinct from its global transactions, China's trade surplus has decreased since 2008 mainly as a consequence of the sharp U.S. recession. But the bilateral trade balance still represents about one-third of the reduced U.S. annual trade deficit of about $550 billion (down by more than 20 percent from prerecession levels) and a somewhat larger fraction of the 2009 U.S. annual current account deficit of about $540 billion. The difference in China's shares of the respective balances reflects China's increased earnings from its prior foreign investments, including its large holdings of U.S. Treasury bonds and other government obligations. These holdings, amounting to approximately $1.5 trillion, generate earnings between $40 billion and $45 billion annually and constitute a substantial increment to China's bilateral current account surplus with the United States.[5]

The increased importance in China's international accounts of its net earnings from foreign investments—including investments in U.S. government obligations—has been somewhat obscured by misinformed criticism of China's alleged "manipulation" of the yuan's exchange peg to the U.S. dollar. The criticism is based on a mistaken premise that China's trade and current account imbalances with the United States result from China's failure to let the yuan appreciate rela-

---

[5] "Trade, Exchange Rates, Budget Balances, and Interest Rates," *The Economist*, April 17, 2010, p. 106.

tive to the dollar. According to this argument, instead of the prevailing rate of about 6.7 yuan per dollar, the "true" exchange value of the yuan would be considerably higher, perhaps 4 or 5 yuan per dollar (that is, 1 yuan would be worth 20–25 U.S. cents, rather than 15 cents), thereby tending to increase China's imports from and reduce its exports to the United States.

The criticism is mistaken because, as long as China's aggregate domestic savings rate substantially exceeds its domestic investment rate (recall our earlier discussion of the drivers of China's economic growth), China will maintain a surplus in its global accounts. Regardless of the short-term, transitory effects of changes in the yuan-dollar exchange rate, China's bilateral accounts with the United States will continue to show surpluses reflecting well-established and durable bilateral trade connections between U.S. and Chinese firms and their joint ventures.[6]

Another facet of the international economic and financial environment that affects China's foreign investments is the recent and perhaps growing controversy over possible diminution, or even replacement, of the U.S. dollar's role as the principal global medium of exchange. Were this change to happen, global demand for dollars would shrink, the dollar's exchange value would erode, and the value of China's holdings of dollar assets, including U.S. companies, would fall.

Numerous factors associated with the global financial crisis have contributed to this controversy. These include the $700 billion Troubled Assets Recovery Program, established to relieve the stressed balance sheets of major U.S. banks, and the large U.S. economic stimulus package in 2009.[7] The U.S. economy has received a much larger injec-

---

[6]   See Charles Wolf, Jr., "A Smarter Approach to the Yuan," *Policy Review*, April–May, 2011. In theory, it would be possible for China to have surpluses in its global current accounts and deficits bilaterally with the United States. In practice, this is unlikely. Established trade linkages between China's exporting and importing firms and those in the United States—at least in the short to medium term—make it most likely that bilateral surpluses with the United States will continue to be a major component of China's continuing global current account surpluses, although the size of the bilateral surpluses may decrease.

[7]   At $787 billion, the U.S. stimulus package was, in relative terms, less than half the share of U.S. GDP that China's own stimulus package was of its GDP: 6 percent and 14 percent, respectively.

tion of liquidity and U.S. budget deficits to finance domestic programs, bailouts of the automobile industry, the troubled U.S. banking system, and the "conservatorships" of near-bankrupted, government-sponsored enterprises (i.e., Fannie Mae and Freddie Mac). The resulting surge of U.S. federal debt and the expansion of the U.S. money supply have heightened international concerns about the future stability of the dollar and its reliability as the principal international reserve currency. This in turn has led China and some other countries to argue that currencies other than the dollar, or a mixed basket of currencies, or the special drawing rights (SDR) used as an accounting standard by the International Monetary Fund (IMF), or the Chinese yuan itself should be considered as replacements for the dollar.

Such reforms in the international financial environment are unlikely in the short term. The yuan's prospects as an international reserve currency are remote as long as the yuan remains incompletely convertible, and China's policymakers have repeatedly stipulated that capital transactions are unlikely to be fully convertible for the indefinite future. Furthermore, the role of SDR is likely to remain limited to their function as an accounting device. Even in this role, SDR are subject to periodic changes in the weighting of the component currencies (i.e., dollars, yen, euros, and sterling) as their respective shares of international trade change. Nevertheless, in the medium to longer term, maintenance of the dollar's central role in international finance is subject to question and to challenge. How the challenge is met will depend on various factors, including, especially, the maintenance of open rather than protectionist U.S. trade policies, effective management of the swollen federal debt, and whether this management averts serious inflation and serious depreciation of the U.S. dollar during the next three or four years.

The preceding discussion summarizes some of the principal and changing aspects of the global financial environment in which China's foreign investments will evolve, and to which the prospective recipient countries will respond by encouragement, abridgement, resistance, or other measures.

# CHAPTER THREE

# China's Recent and Prospective Foreign Investments

China's foreign investment strategy is distinctive, selective, and flexible. It is distinctive in that it reflects both the central government and ruling party's broad national priorities that prominently include the salient need of the Chinese economy to sustain high rates of economic growth. The distinctive role of the central government is a consequence of the fact that China's major foreign capital transactions require approval by the SAB and the SAFE, both of which are accountable to the State Council. When competing claims arise to use China's foreign investments to help in meeting the demands of the economy, the military, and the economy's technological advancement, they are resolved or reconciled through and by these institutions with a final decision made at the top of the institutional pyramid.

That China's foreign investment strategy is selective is evident from the conspicuous differences among China's investments in the United States, Europe, Asia, and the rest of the world during the 2007–2009 period. As we will discuss later in this chapter, in some instances China's foreign investments focus on realizing stable returns or on higher, if more volatile, returns. In other instances, the focus is on acquiring companies with large oil, gas, and other mineral resource holdings, or companies with advanced technology, laboratories, and testing capabilities. And in still other instances, the companies that

China has sought and acquired are ones with evident financial experience, connections, and know-how.[1]

The strategy's flexibility is suggested in recent policy pronouncements by Prime Minister Wen Jiabao and Minister of Commerce Chen Deming. Both leaders expressed their encouragement for expanded investment abroad, especially investment by China's "most capable" companies; a notable outlier in the flexibility domain is a previous expression of Chinese interest in acquiring a substantial stake in the Cleveland Cavaliers basketball team.[2]

## China's Investments in the United States, 2007–2009

Notwithstanding frequent Chinese criticism of mounting U.S. budget deficits and the jeopardy this creates for the stability of the U.S. dollar in international markets,[3] China's investments in the United States continue to be predominantly in U.S. Treasury notes and bills and other U.S. government obligations. China's accumulation of these U.S. government assets by the middle of 2009 reached more than $1.5 trillion. Nearly one-third of these holdings—about $450 billion—were accumulated from 2007 through the middle of 2009.[4] China's concerns about the stability of the dollar are understandable in light of the

---

[1]  This period is of particular interest because China's foreign investments rose substantially above the levels in earlier years and did so notwithstanding the financial crisis that struck most severely in 2008. China's global investments in 2007 and 2008 increased threefold above their levels in 2005 and 2006. They have continued to increase in the years since 2009.

[2]  Chen Deming, "Strengthen U.S.-China Trade Ties," *Wall Street Journal*, April 27, 2009; *Business Daily*, update, December 16, 2009.

[3]  See Xinhua Economic News Service, July 22, 2009.

[4]  Authors' estimates based on the following parameters: China's annualized current account surplus in 2007–2009 (first two quarters) = $300 billion/year; 60 percent of this surplus is assumed to be invested in U.S. government obligations = $180 billion/year (although the actual proportion is probably 70 percent, we assume 60 percent in preference for erring on the low side). Hence, for the 2007–2009 period: $180 billion/year × 2.5 years = $450 billion (China's estimated investments in U.S. government obligations); $120 billion/year × 2.5 years = $300 billion (China's estimated investments in other assets in the United States, Europe, Asia, and the rest of the world). Assuming that its holdings of U.S. government obli-

size of its dollar holdings and of prospective additions to them. In any event, China's large and continuing investments in U.S. government securities suggest a keen interest in having in its portfolio a substantial component that can be relied on to generate stable returns and that will continue to be a secure store of value.

China's new investments in U.S.-based companies during the 2007–2009 period reached $25.8 billion, approximately 5 percent of China's investments in U.S. government obligations during the same period. The largest share of investments in U.S. companies was in banking and financial services (78 percent), with the remainder divided among refineries, semiconductors, telecommunications, laboratory testing equipment, auto parts, and miscellaneous other industries. The concentration in banking and financial services provides a means for China to both learn about and establish linkages to broad segments of the U.S. economy. The other components of China's acquisitions of U.S. companies suggest some of the principal sectoral interests motivating its investments.

Table 3.1 summarizes China's investments in the United States by buyer, seller, and industrial sector. As the table shows, investments by Chinese companies, as well as by China's sovereign wealth fund—the China Investment Corporation—and other government and quasi-governmental organizations, such as SAFE and the China International Trust and Development Corporation (CITIC), were concentrated in the financial and business services industries. Although the scale of these investments ($16.8 billion over the 2007–2009 period) is small relative to China's investments in U.S. government obligations over the same period, the reasons for concentration in the financial and business sector investments seem, from China's point of view, compelling. These reasons include the warranted (although disappointed) expectation of high rates of return on investments in these sectors; the pessimistic legacy of the China National Offshore Oil Corporation (CNOOC) case in 2005,[5] which tended to discourage investments in high-

---

gations represent 60 percent of China's total foreign exchange reserves, the latter is estimated as $2.1 trillion ($1.5 trillion × 1.4).

[5]   This case is discussed further in Chapter Four.

Table 3.1
China's Investments in U.S. Companies, 2007–2009: Buyers, Sellers, and Industries

| Year | Buyer | Seller | Industry | Investment ($ millions) |
|------|-------|--------|----------|-------------------------|
| 2007 | Husky Inc. | Lima Refinery | Oil and gas field services | 1,900 |
|  | CITIC | Delta Tech Controls | Electronic components | 10 |
|  | China Investment Corporation (CIC) | Blackstone (12.5%) | Miscellaneous investment | 4,000 |
|  | CIC | Morgan Stanley (7.9%) | Miscellaneous business services | 5,600 |
| Total |  |  |  | 11,510 |
| 2008 | Husky Inc. | Toledo Refinery | Oil and gas services | 2,500 |
|  | Mindray Medical | Datascope Corporation | Electromedical equipment | 202 |
|  | Grace Semiconductors | STM Microelectronics | Electronic components | Not disclosed[a] |
|  | CITIC | Citizens Mutual Telephone | Telecommunications equipment | 33 |
|  | Wuxi Pharmatech | AppTec Lab Services | Testing laboratories | 151 |
|  | Spreadtrum Communications | Quorum Systems | Semiconductors | 7 |
|  | CIC | Visa (<1%) | Business services | 100 |
|  | China Life | Visa (1%) | Business services | 300 |
|  | CIC | JC Flowers | Miscellaneous investment | 4,000 |
|  | SAFE | Texas Pacific Group | Miscellaneous investment | 5,600 |
| Total |  |  |  | 12,893 |
| 2009 | Beijing West Ind. | Delphi Auto Parts | Motor vehicles and parts | 100 |
|  | Airtime DSL | TAG Industries | Lighting equipment | 27 |
|  | Qiaoxing Group | Freescale Semiconductors | Communications equipment | 100 |
|  | CIC | Morgan Stanley (2%) | Business services | 1,200 |
| Total |  |  |  | 1,427 |

SOURCES: Mergerstat; various reports in Xinhua Economic News Service, *Financial Times*, Reuters, *Wall Street Journal*, and other Chinese and U.S. press releases.

NOTES: Percentages shown in parentheses under the column labeled "Seller" indicate the ownership stake acquired by the buyer. The absence of percentages implies 100 percent acquisition.

[a] The value of the Grace investment is omitted from the accessible data sources.

technology companies that China might otherwise have been interested in acquiring; and the plausible expectation by China's policymakers that acquisitions in finance and business services would provide a unique opportunity for Chinese companies to learn about and access a broad range of companies throughout the U.S. economy.

That such broad considerations are important in affecting, and hence in analyzing, the patterns and strategies motivating China's foreign investments in the United States and elsewhere follows from certain special circumstances relating to foreign investment by China. Salient among them is the fact that, since the Chinese yuan is not freely convertible in capital transactions, investment by corporate or individual Chinese investors requires approval by SAB and SAFE. These bodies are accountable to the State Council, and its imprimatur is essential, even if tacit, for foreign investments to be accomplished by any Chinese entity.

In light of these special circumstances, how should one assess the entire portfolio of China's acquisitions of U.S. companies shown in Table 3.1? The question is difficult because the answer is highly dependent on the perspective of the assessor.

For example, if the assessment were made by a professional financial analyst whose perspective would typically focus on achieving a balanced and diversified portfolio, the assessment would stress that the Chinese portfolio is unbalanced by its overweighting of acquisitions in the financial, banking, and business investment sectors; that the portfolio's evident secondary emphasis on oil- and gas-related assets helps only modestly to provide a balancing set of holdings; and that the several smaller acquisitions relating to telecommunications, electronics, and laboratory testing facilities show a small but active reach for technology-related assets that may result in breakthrough payoffs in the future.

On the other hand, if the assessment were made by a professional U.S. national security analyst, the assessment would be cast differently. It would instead argue that the portfolio's emphasis on the financial, banking, and business investment sectors suggests a Chinese interest in acquiring information, contacts, and connections that extend into the wide reaches of the U.S. economy and may reveal useful insights into its strengths and perhaps vulnerabilities; that the oil- and gas-related investments are another among many indicators of China's compelling global interests in enhancing and securing access to energy and other natural resources vital for sustaining its rapid economic growth; and that the smaller acquisitions in technology-related sectors are an indication of a keen Chinese interest in testing how far it may be able to go in trying to access advanced U.S. technologies with possible military as well as other future payoffs, while avoiding the obstructing legacy of the CNOOC contretemps of 2005.

Table 3.1 also shows that China's investments in U.S. companies in 2009 declined sharply from those in the two preceding years. This is a consequence of both the deep recession in the U.S. economy as well as the large losses experienced in the market values of China's U.S. investments that were made in 2007 and 2008.

We expect the scale of China's investments in U.S. companies to rise again in the next few years and the prior pattern of investment concentration in the financial and business services sectors to shift. The reasons for these expectations include China's continuing current account surpluses, emergent opportunities for acquiring a wide range of U.S. companies as a result of their depressed valuations, a growing and probably warranted belief that the CNOOC legacy of U.S. rejection of Chinese investment has attenuated since 2005, and hence receptivity in the United States to acquisitions by financially well-endowed Chinese investors may be higher than in prior years.

These reasons are reflected in a recent pronouncement by China's Minister of Commerce and member of the State Council, Chen Deming, of a new ("Going Out") policy of encouraging capable Chinese companies to invest in the United States.[6] In this context, the term *capable* encompasses the resources, experience, and economic and political connections of Chinese investors presumed to be capable and whose transit through the SAB and SAFE channels is therefore likely to be relatively smooth and swift. Prime Minister Wen Jiabao has more recently endorsed and elaborated on this stance and has stated his

---

[6]   Deming, 2009.

expectation that China's investments in foreign enterprises will grow in coming years.[7]

To further highlight the distinctiveness of China's investments in the United States, Table 3.2 compares them with the pooled investments of five of the largest and most experienced private equity firms: Carlyle Group, Blackstone, Cerberus, Kohlberg-Kravis-Roberts (KKR), and Berkshire Hathaway.[8] Using the PE firms as one standard of comparison with China's investments is admittedly a stretch because the business models guiding the investments of these firms differ so markedly from those that plausibly may guide China's investments.

**Table 3.2**
**Private Equity Investments in U.S. Companies, 2007–2009:**
**Industries and Investments of Five PE Firms**

| Industry | Investment ($ millions) |
|---|---|
| Hotels and motels | 39,934 |
| Real estate investment trusts | 19,332 |
| Construction materials | 10,300 |
| Motor vehicles and car bodies | 7,400 |
| Packaged frozen foods | 7,200 |
| Management consulting services | 7,040 |
| Motor vehicle parts and accessories | 5,575 |
| Skilled nursing care facilities | 4,922 |

SOURCES: Mergerstat; company and trade association reports.

NOTE: Data are pooled for Carlyle, Blackstone, KKR, Cerberus, and Berkshire Hathaway, covering the combined 2007–2009 period.

---

[7] *Financial Times*, FT.com; Jamil Anderlini, "Forex Funds to fuel China Purchases," July 22, 2009. In the context of Premier Wen's remarks, "going out" essentially means that an undisclosed but substantial amount of additional foreign exchange will be available for Chinese companies to use in pursuing foreign acquisitions.

[8] Berkshire Hathaway is a public company, but its major investment activities, which use funds from its insurance business as well as from Berkshire shareholders, are close counterparts to those of the private equity companies in the pooled data set.

For example, PE firms generally have a short- to medium-term invest-ment horizon with a view to a profit-yielding exit within two to five years, whereas Chinese investors may have a longer-term horizon with no obligation to exit in a defined period. Also, PE firms typically have (or believe they have) expert knowledge of the markets in which they are investing, whereas Chinese investors may have more limited market knowledge.

Consequently, for these and other reasons, we would expect the investment patterns and portfolios of Chinese and PE investment to differ sharply. Still, there are at least a few strands that China's invest-ments and those of the PE firms have in common. One strand is that both China and the PE firms strongly prefer full buy-outs or dominant equity acquisitions rather than minority shares in the investments they make. Another is that profitmaking is a compelling aim for both— for the PE firms it is quintessential so they can pay off their investors in the short run; for China's investments it is important in order to replenish funding for future investments, as well as to further the other key objectives discussed above. It is perhaps worth noting, as a passing comment, that the business models associated with hedge firms would be even more of a stretch for comparison with China's investments because hedge firms typically have a much shorter time horizon for quick turnover and exit than do PE firms.

In any event, the PE comparison is of interest because the top-quality PE firms are usually considered to have smart, flexible, and adroit investment managers, and the comparison serves to highlight the composition and magnitude of the differences between China's state-managed investments and those of private international firms.

The equity investments shown in Table 3.2 for the top eight Stan-dard Industrial Code (SIC) sectors of the pooled five PE firms con-stitute almost all (94 percent) of the firms' total investments in U.S. companies ($102.2 billion) during the 2007–2009 period. The contrast with China's investments shown in the preceding table is striking.

- China's U.S. investments are dominated by acquisitions in finance and business services, whereas the PE firms' investments in these sectors are negligible—indeed, as indicated in Table 3.1, several of China's largest U.S. investments were targeted at the financial services firms themselves (e.g., Blackstone, Morgan Stanley).

- China's U.S. investments also show interest in selective high-technology companies, such as laboratories and testing facilities, telecommunications, and semiconductors, whereas the PE firms' main investments avoid these sectors.
- The PE firms' U.S. investments in the 2007–2009 period concentrated on hotels and motels, real estate, construction, and motor vehicles—none of which figure prominently among China's U.S. investments (see Table 3.2).

That the portfolio of China's acquisitions of and investments in U.S. companies differs from that of the pooled private equity firms' acquisitions would not be surprising in light of their differing objectives and business models, as discussed above. However, to test the extent and significance of these differences, we made a crude statistical comparison between the industrial sectors encompassed by China's acquisitions shown in Table 3.1 and those encompassed by the PE firms' acquisitions shown in Table 3.2. Using the SIC numerical designations of the respective acquisitions, the hypothesis we test is that China's acquisitions do not differ from those of the previously mentioned private equity firms. While fully acknowledging the sparseness of the data and the simplicity of the test, we find that this simple hypothesis cannot be rejected.[9]

---

[9] The comparison is based on the SIC numbers of the acquisitions shown in Tables 3.1 and 3.2. Two among the 18 SIC categories covered in the tables are shared by both the PE and Chinese portfolios shown in the table, whereas the full number of SIC three-digit sectors is more than 400. Using a simple $\chi$-square test for the independence of the two sets of acquisitions, the hypothesis that the two sets do not differ cannot be rejected; the result is statistically significant at a 1 percent level. Stated another way, if one thinks of the universe of possible three-digit SICs that either China or PE firms could invest in, then the existence of PE investment in any one SIC category is a statistically significant predictor of a category that is likely to receive investment by China. To state the point another way, most SICs have zero investments from both PE and Chinese investors; so, the fact that PE firms and China both select some of the same SICs occurs with greater frequency than would be expected by chance.

Quite apart from this result, there are several other intriguing aspects of the current and potential connections between U.S. private equity firms and China's foreign investments. While it would be worthwhile for U.S. analysts to understand and explore this matter further, budget and time constraints preclude our doing so in this report.[10]

## China's Investments in Europe, 2007–2009

China's investments in Europe are summarized in Table 3.3.

As Table 3.3 indicates, China's investments in Europe have been concentrated in two sectors: oil and gas, and financial and banking services. The focus on oil and gas reflects the priority accorded to resource security by China's policymakers—a theme that predominates in China's investments in Asia and the rest of the world, as discussed below. In the European context, the oil and gas priority takes the form of acquiring minority shares in some of the world's largest global multinational producers—specifically, BP and Total. For China's investments in Asia and the rest of the world, this predominant priority leads to investments aimed, as far as possible, at acquiring either full ownership or at least a substantial equity share.

The factors explaining China's European investments in financial and banking services are similar to the ones mentioned above as motivating China's investments in the same sector in the United States. These factors include learning about and gaining access to a wide spectrum of European companies and industrial sectors through the lending and securities transactions of financial and banking services com-

---

[10] For example, it is noteworthy that one of China's largest single company investments ($4 billion by the China Investment Corporation) has been for acquisition of a consequential stake in a major PE firm, Blackstone, in 2007 (see Table 3.1). And in 2008, Carlyle, another of the major PE firms, formed an investment partnership with Shandong province—China's second-largest and second-richest province—for a Ren Min Bi fund that will make investments in companies based in the coastal province as well as co-invest with them overseas. The potential for mutual gains by Carlyle and its province partner includes the intellectual property that the Chinese participants may reasonably expect to acquire, as well as the profits that both participants stand to garner from the joint venture. (See "Asia News," *Private Equity International*, Vol. 5, No. 66, June 2008.)

**Table 3.3**

**China's Investments in European Companies, 2007–2009: Buyers, Sellers, and Industries**

| Year | Buyer | Seller | Industry | Investment ($ millions) |
|------|-------|--------|----------|-------------------------|
| 2007 | China Development Bank | Barclays (3%) | Miscellaneous investments | 3,000 |
| | Ping'an Bank | Fortis (4.2%) | Commercial banks and life insurance | 2,700 |
| | ICBC | ICBC Asia (8.2%) | Foreign bank and branches | 245 |
| Total | | | | 5,945 |
| 2008 | SAFE | Total (1.6%) | Crude oil and gas | 2,820 |
| | SAFE | BP (1%) | Crude oil and gas | 2,000 |
| | CNOOC | Norwegian Awilco | Oil and gas services | 2,490 |
| | Bank of China | Swiss Heritage Fund | Miscellaneous investments | 8.7 |
| Total | | | | 7,319 |
| 2009 | SAFE | Total (1.6%) | Crude oil and gas | 705 |

SOURCES: Chinese and European press releases; Mergerstat.

NOTES: The figures in parentheses are the shares of ownership acquired by China's investments. The absence of percentages implies 100 percent acquisition. The 2009 SAFE estimate of investment in Total is the authors' estimate. It is based on prorating small addition to ownership share according to the cost/share ratio of acquisition in 2008. Investment totals may not sum exactly because of rounding.

panies. That said, there are reasons for expecting both the magnitude and the sectoral acquisitions by China's investors in European companies to expand and to widen, respectively.

Expanded investments in Europe are a likely consequence of the continuing large current account surpluses of the Chinese economy discussed above. The broadened scope of investments may be affected as well by China's anticipation that acquisitions aiming at high-technology companies and sectors may encounter less sensitivity and resistance in Europe than similarly targeted acquisitions would encounter in the United States. Quite apart from the sensitivity issue, China's bids and efforts in Europe may have a galvanizing competitive effect on possible mergers and acquisitions in the United States, and the converse may also be true. European and U.S. companies in similar fields may seek, as well as be sought by, infusions of capital from China.

Evidence of a probably broadened span of China's sectoral investments in Europe is provided by European visits in the first quarter of 2009 by two large, financially well-equipped Chinese commercial delegations.[11] The delegations' explicit and conjoined purposes were to identify opportunities for both procurement and investment in telecommunications equipment, electronics, energy-saving technology, pharmaceuticals, automobiles, trains, and machinery. In the midst of depressed economic conditions in Europe, linking procurement contracts in the short run with investment acquisitions thereafter may be particularly effective.

## China's Investments in Asia and the Rest of the World

China's principal investments in Asia and the rest of the world are summarized in Table 3.4.

As Table 3.4 plainly indicates, China's investments in Asia and the rest of the world show a markedly different pattern from its investments in the United States and Europe shown in Tables 3.1 and 3.3. In the 2007–2009 period, China focused its investments in the rest of the world on resource industries, such as oil, gas, copper, iron, lead, and zinc. Moreover, the resource focus reflected in Table 3.4 excludes substantial (i.e., $35 billion) lending by Chinese financial institutions to resource industries in Brazil and Singapore, as well as additional

---

[11] Joe McDonald, "Chinese Go to Europe with $15 Billion to Spend," PharmPro.com, February 24, 2009; "China, Germany Sign $14 B in Trade Deals," *China Daily*, February 26, 2009; "2nd Chinese Shopping Delegation Leaves for Europe," *China Daily*, March 8, 2009.

**Table 3.4**
**China's Investments in Asia and the Rest of World, 2007–2009: Buyers, Sellers, and Industries**

| Year | Buyer | Seller | Industry | Investment ($ millions) |
|---|---|---|---|---|
| 2007 | China Mobile | Paktel | Telecommunications | 460 |
| | Chinalco | Peru Copper | Copper ores | 790 |
| | Sinopec | Iranian National | Oil and gas | 2,000 |
| | Haier | Thailand Refrigerator | Appliances | 20 |
| | Haier | India Refrigerator | Appliances | Not disclosed |
| | ICBC | Seng Heng Bank (Macao) (80%) | Foreign banks | 586 |
| | ICBC | South Africa Standard (20%) | Foreign banks | 5,000 |
| | ICBC | Thai ACL Bank (19%) | Foreign banks | 33 |
| | China Development Bank | PakChina Investment Corporation | Miscellaneous investments | 100 |
| Total | | | | 8,989 |
| 2008 | Chinalco | Toromach Copper Mine | Copper ores | 2,160 |
| | Xinxing and China Metal | Indian JV | Metal mining services | 1,200 |
| | Suntech Power | Japan MSK Solar (33%) | Miscellaneous electricity machinery | 107 |
| | China Aluminum International Engineering | Vietnam bauxite mine | Miscellaneous metal ores | 466 |
| | Shanghai Automotive | Sangyong Automotive (2.1%) | Motor vehicles | 50 |
| | China Merchant Bank | HK Wing Lung Bank (53.1%) | Foreign banking services | 2,500 |
| Total | | | | 6,483 |
| 2009 | China MinMetals | OZ Metals (Australia) | Copper, lead, zinc, other ores | 1,200 |
| | CNPC | Singapore Petroleum Corporation (45.5%) | Oil and gas | 1,000 |
| | Hunan Valin | Fortescue (17%) | Iron ores | 462 |
| | Haier | Prachin Buri Refrigerator Thailand | Appliances | 5 |
| Total | | | | 2,667 |

NOTES: Percentages in parentheses refer to the equity share acquired by China. The absence of percentages implies 100 percent acquisition. Data for 2009 cover only the first four months of the year. ICBC = Industrial and Commercial Bank of China. CNPC = China National Petroleum Corporation.

long-term procurement contracts in Iran and Libya for oil and gas and other resources.[12]

After engaging in numerous conversations with officials and scholars both in China and in the United States, we opine that China's increasing emphasis in the 2007–2009 period on resource investments in the rest of the world is likely to continue in the coming years. The obvious reason is China's continuing and growing demand for basic resources as a consequence of and contributor to sustaining high rates of GDP growth. As the global markets' second-largest importer of crude oil (after the United States and ahead of Japan) and as the largest importer of copper, iron, and other ores, China accords high priority to economic growth, which underlies its emphasis on investment acquisitions in these sectors.

It is not evident whether this policy is wise or optimal. Indeed, to make this determination would require a combined assessment of economic, security, and political considerations that would warrant more time than can be devoted to it here. We offer instead several observations to indicate the complexity involved in reaching a conclusion about whether this is a wise policy.

Whether investing in foreign resources is sensible policy for China depends on whether the future prices of those resources rise or fall relative to those of outputs from investments in other sectors. For example, whether downstream energy prices and, more specifically, the prices of oil and gas rise or fall relative to a broad market basket of goods and services will determine whether current investments in oil and gas production are profitable. On the one hand, rising global GDP will lead to increased demand for energy and hence to expected increases in the relative prices of energy-related resources. On the other hand, major efforts under way to develop alternative energy sources (e.g., not only through wind, solar, biomass, and nuclear sources but also through advanced technologies in nanotechnology), as well as efforts to con-

---

[12] In 2008, PetroBraz borrowed $10 billion from China Development Bank (CDB) and Sinopec. In 2009, a consortium of Chinese lenders—including CDB, China's Export-Import Bank, Sinopec, and CNPC—extended loans totaling $25 billion to Transneft and Rosneft (in Russia and Central Asia) for oil and gas development. China may well convert these loans into equity investments in the coming years.

serve energy and reduce carbon emissions, will tend to lower the same relative prices.

The security dimension of this assessment is no less complex. Whether ownership of resource-producing companies located abroad would place China in a more secure or more vulnerable position is also open to debate. Products that are homogeneous—such as oil, gas, and metal ores—command a single price in international markets, apart from differing transportation costs between points of origin and destination. If China draws on supplies from companies it owns, other consuming countries can draw on remaining global supplies, with the diminished demand from China having less effect on prices than if China were a competing buyer.

The political dimension further complicates the assessment, as amply demonstrated by Chinalco's recent unsuccessful attempt to acquire a 20 percent ownership stake in Australia's Rio Tinto mining corporation.[13] Usually, a foreign investment transaction conducted with reasonable transparency, and voluntarily accepted by both parties to the transaction, can be presumed to redound to their mutual benefit. However, where national sensitivities are engaged, as in the Rio Tinto case, and in CNOOC's attempted acquisition of California's UNOCAL in 2005, the presumed mutual benefit may be offset by concerns over potential future frictions.[14]

In sum, it is uncertain whether aggressive pursuit of what are intended by China to be resource-security acquisitions is a sensible or a misplaced part of China's foreign investment strategy.

---

[13] See Samuel Thawley, "Resource Security Policies of China and Japan: A Case Study of the Iron and Steel Sector," Santa Monica, Calif.: RAND Corporation, unpublished research.

[14] For an interesting comparative analysis of the contrasting policies of China's and Japan's concerns and policies relating to resource security, see Thawley, unpublished research. Although no less concerned with and dependent on imported sources of energy and metal ores, Japan's policies focus more on procurement contracts and project financing and less on foreign corporate acquisitions than do China's policies.

# CHAPTER FOUR

# Assessing Chinese Investments

The preceding chapters have provided background for comparing the magnitudes and sectoral composition of China's investments in the United States, Europe, Asia, and the rest of the world. In light of this background, we begin this chapter with several observations concerning the broad patterns of China's foreign investments. This leads to our development of a methodology for evaluating potential new investments to assist in identifying the positive and negative factors that may be associated with these investments.

## Patterns of China's Investments

First, with the world's largest holdings of foreign exchange reserves, China has been making foreign investments to advance multiple objectives: maintaining a stable exchange rate that facilitates China's exports; securing access to and ownership of natural resources to sustain its rapid economic growth; and acquiring foreign technologies and know-how to advance these objectives as well as to further its national security interests.

Second, China has demonstrated an ability and flexibility that enable it to take advantage of differing opportunities for acquisitions in different countries.

Third, China's large and growing buying power and its world-wide sourcing may place it in a strategic position capable of playing the United States against other sellers and enabling it to partition acquisition of targeted technologies into different investment packages adapted to differing circumstances in different countries.

Fourth, several studies, apart from our own, claim that over the past few decades, the emphasis accorded by China to political and security objectives has gradually given way to the primacy of commercial interests.[1]

## U.S. Response

These observations have implications for U.S. responses to Chinese investments in the United States.

First, a concern lest China outmaneuver the United States, as mentioned above, is one reason why Chapter Three examined China's worldwide investments in order to have a full picture that will better enable the United States to respond effectively in averting national security risks. A wider-angle lens on China's investment patterns can help ensure that responses are informed and effective.

Second, the United States traditionally, and the National Security Act of 2007 specifically, have construed "critical technologies" to mean technologies essential to national defense. As China's acquisitions spread to many more sectors a question arises: Are critical technologies only those critical to national security[2] or are technologies that are critical for economic advancement also important from a national security perspective?

---

[1]   For example, one study surveyed 296 member companies of the China Chamber of International Commerce and concluded that the motivation for China's outward investment will increasingly be driven by market considerations rather than policy directives. (See Yuen Pau Woo and Kenny Zhang, "China Goes Global: The Implications of Chinese Outward Direct Investment," Asia-Pacific Foundation of Canada, 2006.) However, from the standpoint of our study, it does not matter whether or not one agrees with this finding concerning the trend as long as it is acknowledged that both central government policy guidance as well as business potential will be critical considerations for China's investments in the foreseeable future.

[2]   Committee on Foreign Investment in the United States, *Annual Report to Congress*, Public Version, Appendix A, December 2008.

Third, critical technologies might therefore include not only the financial and business sector and the energy sector that we study in this chapter but many other sectors as well if these technologies are shown to have a critical effect on economic security as well as on defense.

Fourth, this chapter develops a decision-tree analytic methodology to help identify proposed Chinese acquisitions, or acquisitions by other countries, that create national security concerns and to help devise plans for mitigating or, if necessary, blocking them entirely.

Before developing a way to evaluate proposed Chinese investments in U.S. companies, we consider the meaning of "critical technologies" and "national security." The breadth of each term creates ambiguities, invites different interpretations, and yields different implications.

## Critical Technologies and National Security: Background Legislation and Administration

The Foreign Investment and National Security Act of 2007 (FINSA) amended section 721 of the Defense Production Act of 1950[3] to correct perceived deficiencies in the process by which that statute reconciled national security and promotion of foreign investment.[4] FINSA does not define national security, other than noting that the term also includes issues relating to homeland security.[5] However, FINSA mentions factors that are particularly germane to this study, such as "potential national security-related effects on United States critical infrastructure, including major energy assets"; "the long-term projection of United States requirements for sources of energy and other critical resources and materials"; and "the relationship of (the investment's

---

[3] Defense Production Act of 1950, 50 United States Code (U.S.C.) App. §2170, September 8, 1950.

[4] Foreign Investment and National Security Act of 2007, Public Law (P.L.) 110-49, July 26, 2007.

[5] *Federal Register*, "Guidance Concerning the National Security Review Conducted by the Committee on Foreign Investment in the United States," Office of Investment Security, Department of the Treasury, Vol. 73, No. 236, December 8, 2008b, p. 74569.

origin) country with the United States, specifically on its record on cooperating in counter-terrorism efforts."[6]

In FINSA, "the term 'critical technologies' means critical technology, critical components, or critical technology items essential to national defense."[7] This law then mandates that the government identify in the federal regulations promulgated to implement the statute a list of which technologies, components, and items fall under this definition.

We cite these somewhat broader definitions because they are similar to the one employed in this study. We construe the effects of foreign investment on a nation's economic security to be no less important than the effects on a nation's defense security. Moreover, we define "critical technologies" as technologies, products, and services that are important to national defense or the national economy. The term includes both existing technologies and those still under development.[8]

Moreover, during the process of writing the FINSA regulations, the Department of the Treasury solicited public comment. In his comment, Senator Jim Webb wrote (regarding proposed rule 800.207), "The proposed rule should take into consideration the importance of economic security when defining national security."[9] However, the final regulations did not do so. In fact, in its section-by-section analysis of the new regulations, the Department of the Treasury and the interagency committee that wrote the regulations explicitly rejected this suggestion: "The Committee will continue its practice of focus-

---

[6]  Foreign Investment and National Security Act of 2007.

[7]  Defense Production Act of 1950.

[8]  In this study, we follow a FINSA amendment stipulating that if the parties to a transaction file a voluntary notice, the notice shall describe "articles and services (including those under development) that may be designated or determined in future to be defense designated or determined in future to be defense articles or defense services."

[9]  Senator Jim Webb, *Webb: Strengthen Proposed Rules Governing Foreign Government Investment in the United States*, press release, June 9, 2008.

ing narrowly on genuine national security concerns alone, not broader economic or other national interests."[10]

In this study, we include the economic dimension as warranting explicit consideration. We note that President Barack Obama's first Presidential Policy Directive states:

> [T]he NSC [National Security Council] shall advise and assist me in integrating all aspects of national security policy as it affects the United States—domestic, foreign, military, intelligence, and economic in conjunction with the National Economic Council.[11]

When a law or regulation calls for an assessment of the effects on national security, our study construes this to include both defense and economic dimensions. Economic crises and stresses not only are national security concerns in their own right but also may have serious national security implications pertaining to defense. Primary or secondary firms in the defense industrial base may be decimated. Support for U.S. forces engaged abroad may be delayed or weakened. The military establishments of allied countries may be further eroded, and political and security instability may be aggravated. Thus, a review of a foreign acquisition should examine whether it could some day lead to hardship affecting U.S. economic well-being and be detrimental to U.S. physical security.

Both broad and narrow interpretations have been ascribed to critical technologies and national security at different times and by different agencies. Indeed, different interpretations have been evident not only in different administrations but in different departments and agencies within these administrations. We are inclined to adopt a broad interpretation that includes, for example, the benefits to the U.S. economy and U.S. infrastructure that may result from foreign capital investment, along with risks that may be envisaged from such investment.

---

[10] *Federal Register*, "Regulations Pertaining to Mergers, Acquisitions, and Takeovers by Foreign Persons," Codified at 31 CFR Part 800, November 21, 2008a, p. 70705.

[11] Presidential Policy Directive 1, The White House, February 13, 2009.

Therefore, we propose a method that enables analysts and their principals to express, weigh, and resolve differing interpretations and judgments about risks and benefits based on the facts of particular cases, both in the past and in the future. Our definition of risks and benefits and our method of assessing security risks and benefits (particularly pertaining to Chinese investments in U.S. companies) could potentially be used with further development as the basis for changes in existing review procedures relating to foreign investments in the United States or other countries.

In developing a methodology for assessing national security risks and benefits, we reviewed 20 proposed Chinese investments from 2000 to 2008 and supplemented these by considering several other possible proposals in the financial, business, and energy sectors. Although we describe the methodology below, we have refrained from including the detailed case studies in this monograph.

## Analytic Methodology for Assessing National Security Risks and Benefits

The analytic methodology we have developed for assessing foreign investments in U.S. companies or companies in other countries is a modified decision-tree analysis consisting of a series of steps, some requiring simultaneous decisions and others requiring successive ones (see Figure 4.1). When the borderline between affirmative (approval) and negative (disapproval) decisions is thin, one would have to consider simultaneously the factors shown in multiple boxes of Figure 4.1 so that the cumulative weights would more clearly tip the decision one way or the other.

For a proposed investment transaction, the first question to be addressed is whether the targeted company provides critical technologies. We designate companies that have such technologies as "leading" companies. They can be large in terms of market value, market share, or earnings. Or, whether small or large, they may possess cutting-edge expertise important to national defense or the national economy.

**Figure 4.1**
**Steps for Assessing National Security Risks and Benefits from Foreign Investments**

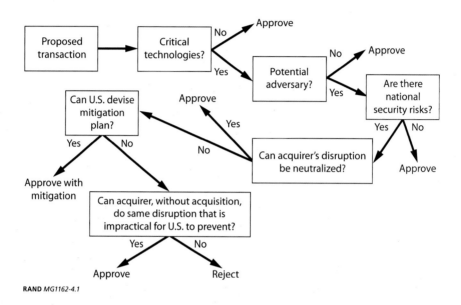

RAND *MG1162-4.1*

If the targeted company is not a leader in the field, we infer that the acquisition would warrant approval. On the other hand, if the company does not pass this decision node, a question still arises whether the foreign acquirer is domiciled in a potentially adversarial country or is a potential adversary, or whether the acquired critical technology or service can eventually be diverted to or misused by a potentially adversarial country or person. If the answer is negative, the transaction can be approved.

Another consideration specific to the United States, as stipulated in FINSA, relates to the acquiring country's cooperation with the United States in counterterrorism efforts. Such cooperation may warrant a favorable judgment relating to China. But if the critical technology or service can fall into the hands of terrorists, the proposed acquisition should be disallowed or an appropriate mitigation plan should be devised.

The decision analysis requires assessing whether the acquisition could damage target country national security and, if so, the scale of such damage. This damage might be military or economic. If the expected damage is negligible, the transaction can be approved. If the likelihood and expected amount of damage are significant, one needs to ask the following questions.

**Can the Acquirer's Disruption Be Neutralized?** If the acquirer in the future decides to withhold the critical technology or service from the company's home country, can other companies pick up the slack and neutralize the supply disruption that would ensue?[12] Also, if an acquiring country were to use the critical technology or service to improve its military capability, does the home country have a way to neutralize that capability? If the answers to these questions are affirmative, the acquirer's hostile action would not cause sizable harm.

**Can the Target Company's Country Devise a Mitigation Plan?** If the answer is affirmative, then it is important that the mitigation plan be carefully designed and effective. For example, the acquirer might be required to divest itself of a subsidiary possessing the critical technology or service. Another possible mitigation measure is to limit the acquirer's voting rights and board seats, thereby preventing it from controlling the company.

Generally, it is not possible to conduct a cost-benefit analysis on foreign investment because national security risks and benefits[13] usually cannot be measured in the same units. We propose to start with

---

[12] An example can clarify this point. Foreign ownership of a U.S. airline cannot exceed 49 percent equity and 25 percent voting rights. However, let us assume that this restriction is lifted. When an airline encounters flight cancellations, other airlines can step in and take care of the affected passengers. Thus, the disruption is neutralized. In the case of investment, if the Chinese acquired a U.S. airline and later sought to discontinue service in the United States, its ticket holders could switch to other airlines. If the acquired airline refused to reimburse other airlines, the Federal Aviation Administration could impose a fine sufficient to cause it to change course. Thus, the disruption would be tolerable and a boycott would be unlikely. The low likelihood of a boycott and the minor effects it would have should make this a nonissue when considering the proposed transaction.

[13] As to assessing the national security benefits, we use a broad definition of critical technologies, to include those that contribute to "strong national defense, improved economic competitiveness, a rising standard of living, improved public health, and energy indepen-

a risk assessment as described in Figure 4.1 but to capture the benefits in the mitigation plan. For the U.S. case, there are no provisions in FINSA, or in other implementing regulations, for incorporating the benefits of a specific transaction into a risk-mitigation agreement. The main provision safeguarding the investment environment is that the mitigation measures must be carefully tailored to respond to a specific risk. In our methodology, we suggest that, in addition to mitigating risks, the mitigation plan should be designed to retain benefits, whenever possible.

**Can the Acquirer, Without Acquisition, Create Disruption That the United States Cannot Prevent?** If an effective mitigation plan cannot be devised, a chance for approval may still remain. If the acquisition were denied, the potential investor might still be able to use other ways to create the same disruption, and the United States might be unable to block it. For example, if the United States were concerned that a prospective acquirer could use an acquired commercial bank to finance illicit activities, such as espionage in the United States, disapproving the acquisition would not eliminate the threat. The acquirer could instead use existing banking branches in the United States to finance such activities.[14] Thus, approval of the transaction could take into consideration that foreign banking branches in the United States have long been permitted and cannot be eliminated. If banks are not adequately regulated to prevent threat financing, Congress should consider appropriate procedures and regulations for both domestic banks and foreign branches to prevent such activities.[15]

---

dence," as mentioned in the introduction to this chapter. We treat these contributions from acquisitions as incremental national security benefits.

[14] For example, Chinese spies and others seeking to engage in illicit activities in the United States could open accounts in a Chinese-acquired U.S. bank. China's government could then wire money to their accounts to fund their activities.

[15] This enhancement of prevention can be enacted through amendments to existing acts, as discussed below.

## The General Principle of Reciprocity

It can be argued that reciprocity is contrary to broad U.S. policy, which strives for open, competitive, and nondiscriminatory trade and investment transactions. Reiteration of this policy is expressed in a recent statement by Treasury Secretary Timothy Geithner:

> As we go through the severe stresses of this crisis, we must not turn our backs on open trade and investment. . . . The United States, China, and the other members of the G20 have committed to not resort to protectionist measures by raising trade and investment barriers. . . .[16]

Although the United States generally and strongly favors liberal trade and investment policies, policy compromises have been made occasionally when compelling circumstances arise. The U.S. levy of a special tariff on imports of automobile tires from China is a recent case in point.[17]

We suggest that the principle of reciprocity can be invoked without seriously affecting the general U.S. policy of favoring liberal trade and investment markets. The United States is currently more open and accessible to foreign investment than is China. Nevertheless, U.S. assertion of the reciprocity principle might be expected to encounter some initial objections and criticism from China. Such objections are not likely to be serious or enduring because China's own restrictions are more extensive and constraining than any the United States might apply. Indeed, prudent consideration of reciprocity may encourage China to adopt reciprocal measures that would be more open and liberal than those it currently maintains.

Foreign companies in China are restricted from entering "strategic and sensitive" industries relating to China's national security, although

---

[16] Timothy Geithner, Secretary of the Treasury, speech given at Peking University, China, June 1, 2009.

[17] Jonathan Weisman, "Obama Sets Tire Tariffs on China," *Wall Street Journal*, September 12, 2009.

without specification of the industries or the scope of the restrictions.[18] Foreign investments in Chinese publications, broadcasting, media, and various Internet-based businesses are prohibited.[19] At the same time, China encourages foreign investment in high-technology, equipment manufacturing, and new materials industries but not in traditional manufacturing industries in which China already has "mature technologies and relatively strong production capability."[20]

The United States and China have dissimilar restrictions on foreign investments in particular sectors and subsectors. China does not encourage foreign investments in mature technologies for fear of risks to its "national economic security," and the United States does not encourage Chinese investments in high technologies that might create national security risks. With reciprocal understanding and mutual respect by both countries for their differing concerns and interests, both can achieve their objectives for foreign investments while safeguarding their national interests. Clarifying the concerns of both countries and mitigating instances where their concerns conflict would likely improve the overall investment climates in both countries.[21]

---

[18] Xin Huang, "China Issues New Guide for Foreign Investment," China.com, November 7, 2007.

[19] "Foreign Direct Investment (FDI)," U.S./China media brief, n.d.

[20] Huang, 2007.

[21] As we discuss below, mitigation agreements, if needed, can be designed to attain this favorable environment for foreign investments in both countries.

# CHAPTER FIVE

# Conclusions, Implications, and Guidelines for Further Research

In his opening remarks to launch the first U.S.-China strategic and economic dialogue on July 27, 2009, President Obama observed:

> The relationship between the United States and China will shape the 21st Century. . . . The United States and China share mutual interests. If we advance those interests through cooperation, our people will benefit. And the world will be better off, because our ability to partner with each other is a pre-requisite for progress on many of the most pressing global challenges.[1]

In the evolving global economy, China's large and growing financial resources are propelled by having the world's largest trade balance and the largest current account balance—trends that are likely to continue, although they might diminish somewhat and fluctuate during the next half-dozen years. The result will increase China's influence in the global economy and strengthen its bargaining power in its quests for companies and resources abroad, including those in the United States. In commenting on the U.S.-China strategic and economic dialogue, two U.S. commentators not usually known for being particularly friendly toward China observed a subtle shift in power between China and the United States, one in which the Chinese are showing a

---

[1]  See Mark Landler and David Sanger, "China Seeks Assurances That U.S. Will Cut Its Deficit," *New York Times*, July 29, 2009.

new assertiveness as they seek to protect their huge investment (in U.S. government securities).[2]

As both a consequence of and a contributor to these trends, China's attempts to make additional investments in U.S. companies are likely to grow substantially in the coming years. Many, and indeed most, of these acquisitions will be mutually beneficial to the United States as well to China. Where they might not be beneficial, the methodology we have developed for assessing potential risks as well as benefits can contribute to better understanding and provide guidelines for further analysis. The methodology can be used to facilitate these processes.

Furthermore, this methodology can also help in drafting a mitigation plan for any proposed transaction that raises security concerns. It can also be used for assessing potential benefits to the United States from a proposed acquisition so that the risks can be alleviated while the broad national security and other benefits are retained.

Reciprocity should be a key consideration in U.S. approval of Chinese investment in U.S. companies. However, because the United States and China do not have the same needs and concerns, the reciprocity does not have to be applied strictly and narrowly, such as bank versus bank or energy company versus energy company. Both countries should aim to make comparable the overall climates, regulations, and outcomes for foreign investments.

From discussions the authors have had with government officials and scholars both in China and in the United States, we conclude that recalling and invoking the principle of reciprocity in devising mitigation plans or other remedial measures would likely induce win-win outcomes while avoiding losses to either party. During the past two decades, China has acquired considerable experience in both encouraging and circumscribing foreign investment within China, including by U.S. investors. China's experience and practice have included restricting foreign equity investment to nonvoting "B" stock, constraining the proportion of ownership that foreign investors could acquire in Chinese companies, and limiting the number and size of foreign firms'

---

[2]   See Landler and Sanger, 2009.

financial platforms in China's capital markets. Reciprocity provides ample grounds for expecting cooperative and compliant response by China to U.S. formulation of creative mitigation plans to deal with proposed acquisition of U.S. companies that may entail security risks.

We expect the number and scale of Chinese investments in U.S. companies to rise in the next few years and the pattern of these expanded investments—while still including further investment in the financial and business services sector—to shift toward other sectors. The reasons for this expected shift include the losses Chinese investors have thus far sustained from concentrating investments in the financial and business sectors, the newly emerging opportunities for acquiring a wide range of U.S. companies as a result of their depressed valuations, and a probably warranted belief by China's policymakers (i.e., SAB and SAFE) that U.S. receptivity to acquisitions by financially well-endowed Chinese investors may be somewhat higher than in prior years.

Turning to China's investments in Europe, the discussion in Chapter Three shows that the pattern of these investments in 2007–2009 exhibits concentration in two sectors: namely, oil and gas, and financial and business services. We expect that China's investments in Europe will continue in these two broad sectors while expanding to certain other sectors as well. Expanded investments in Europe are a likely consequence of China's continued large current account surpluses, as discussed in Chapters Two and Three. At the same time, we expect these expanded investments to aim at acquiring high-technology companies in Europe whose acquisition may encounter (or may be expected by China to encounter) less sensitivity and resistance than similarly targeted acquisitions might encounter in the United States. China's opportunity to benefit from market-based competition among companies based in Europe and the United States will be a prominent part of this process.

Thus, a wider-angle lens for tracking China's foreign investments would be useful. China's investments in European companies should be viewed with a lens that has both a wider angle and is no less acute than the lens applied to viewing China's acquisition of U.S. companies. Indeed, the relevance of interactions between Chinese acquisitions in Europe and those in the United States is important both for "tipping point" reasons relating to specific systems and technologies, as well as for broader reasons.[3]

Our recommendation is the same concerning China's investments in Asia and the rest of the world. As discussed in Chapter Three, China's investment focus in Asia and the rest of the world has been in resource industries, such as oil, gas, copper, iron, lead, and zinc. In turn, this focus on resource security is viewed within China as deriving from the high priority that China's policymakers accord to economic growth and its presumed requirement for secure supplies of critical materials.

The validity of China's policy in this regard is debatable, as are China's efforts to expand such investments in Asia and the rest of the world. That said, it may also be noted that such investments may indirectly benefit the United States, as another principal importer of these commodities.

In any event, the wider-angle lens that the U.S. analytic community could use is important from the standpoint of knowing whether and when a series of Chinese investments might lead to China's acquisition of quasi-monopoly power. Such power might be exercised over valuable ores and other resources, for example, which in turn might create vulnerabilities for the U.S. economy and for U.S. national security. The wider view can help in anticipating and forestalling such outcomes.

---

[3]  This refers to the acquisition of a component technology that, taken together with other component technologies already available to or under the control of a hostile foreign entity, could then enable that foreign entity to exploit or control the technology application.

# Bibliography

"2nd Chinese Shopping Delegation Leaves for Europe," *China Daily*, March 8, 2009.

Anderlini, Jamil, "Forex Funds to fuel China Purchases," July 22, 2009.

"Asia News," *Private Equity International*, Vol. 5, No. 66, June 2008.

Bank Secrecy Act, 31 CFR, Part 103, 1970.

Buckley, Peter, Adam Cross, Hui Tan, Liu Xin, and Hinrich Voss, "Historic and Emergent Trends in Chinese Outward Direct Investment," *Management International Review*, December 2008.

*Business Daily*, update, December 16, 2009.

*The Catalogue for the Guidance of Foreign Investment Industries*, amended 2007.

Chen, Shuxun, and Charles Wolf, Jr., *China, the United States, and the Global Economy*, Santa Monica, Calif.: RAND Corporation, MR-1300-RC, 2001. As of April 26, 2010:
http://www.rand.org/pubs/monograph_reports/MR1300.html

Cheng, Allen, "Inside China Investment Corp.," *Institutional Investor* (International Edition), Vol. 33, No. 8, 2008, pp. 72–79.

"China, Germany Sign $14 B in Trade Deals," *China Daily*, February 26, 2009.

Clark, Harry, and Lisa Wang, "Foreign Investment and National Security," *China Business Review*, Vol. 35, No. 1, January/February 2008.

Committee on Foreign Investment in the United States, *Annual Report to Congress*, Public Version, December 2008.

———, *Annual Report to Congress*, Public Version, 2009.

Communications Act of 1934, 47 U.S.C., §151, 1934.

Defense Production Act of 1950, 50 U.S.C. App. §2170, September 8, 1950.

Deming, Chen, "Strengthen U.S.-China Trade Ties," *Wall Street Journal*, April 27, 2009.

Deng, Ping, "Outward Investment by Chinese MNCs: Motivations and Implications," *Business Horizons*, Vol. 47, No. 3, May–June 2004, pp. 8–16.

*Federal Register*, "Regulations Pertaining to Mergers, Acquisitions, and Takeovers by Foreign Persons," Codified at 31 CFR Part 800, November 21, 2008a.

————, "Guidance Concerning the National Security Review Conducted by the Committee on Foreign Investment in the United States," Office of Investment Security, Department of the Treasury, Vol. 73, No. 236, December 8, 2008b.

*Financial Times*, FT.com.

"Foreign Direct Investment (FDI)," U.S./China media brief, n.d.

Foreign Investment and National Security Act of 2007, P. L. 110-49, July 26, 2007.

Geithner, Timothy, Secretary of the Treasury, speech given at Peking University, China, June 1, 2009. As of April 8, 2010:
http://www.america.gov/st/texttrans-english/2009/June/20090601160915xjsnom mis0.9644281.html

Huang, Xin, "China Issues New Guide for Foreign Investment," China.com, November 7, 2007. As of April 21, 2010:
http://english.china.com/zh_cn/news/china/11020307/20071108/14451967.html

Huang, Yasheng, *Selling China: Foreign Direct Investment During the Reform Era*, Cambridge, UK: Cambridge University Press, 2003.

International Emergency Economic Powers Act, U.S.C., Title 50, P.L. 95-223, Chapter 35, 1977.

International Money Laundering Abatement and Anti-Terrorist Financing Act of 2001, Title III of P.L. 107-56, December 4, 2001.

Landler, Mark, and David Sanger, "China Seeks Assurances That U.S. Will Cut Its Deficit," *New York Times*, July 29, 2009.

Leigh, Lamin, and Richard Podpiera, *The Rise of Foreign Investment in China's Banks: Taking Stock*, Washington, D.C.: International Monetary Fund, Working Paper No. 06/292, December 2006.

Lewis, James A., "New Objectives for CFIUS: Foreign Ownership, Critical Infrastructure, and Communications Interception," *Federal Communications Law Journal*, Vol. 57, June 6, 2005, pp. 457–478.

McDonald, Joe, "Chinese Go to Europe with $15 Billion to Spend," PharmPro. com, February 24, 2009. As of April 26, 2010:
http://www.pharmpro.com/News/2009/02/Chinese-Go-To-Europe-With-$15-billion-To-Spend/

Money Laundering Control Act of 1986, 18 U.S.C., §1956 and §1957, 1986.

Nanto, Dick K., James K. Jackson, Wayne M. Morrison, and Lawrence Kumins, *China and the CNOOC Bid for Unocal: Issues for Congress*, CRS Report for Congress, RL33093, September 15, 2005.

International Law Office, *New Rules on Foreign Investment in Chinese Securities Companies*, June 17, 2008. As of June 12, 2009: http://www.internationallawoffice.com/Newsletters/Detail.aspx?g=61c9f77a-da8d-4753-b721-353f19049151

Office of the Under Secretary of Defense for Intelligence, *Policy Guidance for Foreign Ownership, Control, or Influence (FOCI)*, Directive-Type Memorandum (DTM) 09-019, September 2, 2009.

Overholt, William H., *The Rise of China: How Economic Reform Is Creating a New Superpower*, London and New York: W. W. Norton & Company, Inc., 1993.

————, *Asia, America, and the Transformation of Geopolitics*, New York: Cambridge University Press, 2008.

*Photovoltaic Technology Incubator Selections*, DOE Solar Energy Technologies Program, September 26, 2008. As of April 8, 2010: http://www1.eere.energy.gov/solar/pdfs/sai_pv_incubator_doe_prospectus.pdf

Presidential Policy Directive 1, The White House, February 13, 2009.

*QinetiQ's Zephyr UAV Exceeds Official World Record for Longest Duration Unmanned Flight*, news release, September 10, 2007.

Rawski, Thomas G., "What's Happening to China's GDP Statistics?" *China Economic Review*, Vol. 12, No. 4, December 2001.

*Report on U.S. Critical Technology Companies: Report to Congress on Foreign Acquisition of and Espionage Activities against U.S. Critical Technology Companies*, September 2007.

*Report to Congress on Foreign Acquisition of and Espionage Activities against U.S. Critical Technology Companies*, December 28, 2006.

Rosen, Daniel, and Thilo Hanemann, *China's Changing Outbound Foreign Direct Investment Profile: Drivers and Policy Implications*, Washington, D.C.: Peterson Institute for International Economics, Number PB09-14, June 2009.

Thawley, Samuel, "Resource Security Policies of China and Japan: A Case Study of the Iron and Steel Sector," Santa Monica, Calif.: RAND Corporation, unpublished research, 2010.

The People's Bank of China Decree No. 1, 2006.

"The World in Figures, 2010," *The Economist*, 2009.

"Trade, Exchange Rates, Budget Balances, and Interest Rates," *The Economist*, April 17, 2010, p. 106.

USA PATRIOT Act (Uniting and Strengthening America by Providing Appropriate Tools Required to Intercept and Obstruct Terrorism), October 2001.

Webb, Jim, Senator, *Webb: Strengthen Proposed Rules Governing Foreign Government Investment in the United States*, press release, June 9, 2008.

Weisman, Jonathan, "Obama Sets Tire Tariffs on China," *Wall Street Journal*, September 12, 2009.

Wolf, Charles, Jr., *Looking Backward and Forward: Policy Issues in the Twenty-First Century*, Stanford, Calif.: Hoover Institution Press, 2008.

———, "A Smarter Approach to the Yuan," *Policy Review*, April–May 2011.

Wolf, Charles, Jr., K. C. Yeh, Benjamin Zycher, Nicholas Eberstadt, and Sung-Ho Lee, *Fault Lines in China's Economic Terrain*, Santa Monica, Calif.: RAND Corporation, MR-1686-NA/SRF, 2003. As of April 21, 2010: http://www.rand.org/pubs/monograph_reports/MR1686.html

Woo, Yuen Pau, and Kenny Zhang, "China Goes Global: The Implications of Chinese Outward Direct Investment," Asia-Pacific Foundation of Canada, 2006.

World Bank, *World Bank Indicators Database*, September 15, 2009a.

———, *World Bank Indicators Database*, October 7, 2009b.

Xinhua Economic News Service, July 22, 2009.